BREAK THE RULES
AND GET THE PART

THE APPLAUSE ACTING SERIES

BREAK THE RULES AND GET THE PART

Thirty Monologues For Women

LIRA KELLERMAN

APPLAUSE
THEATRE & CINEMA BOOKS
AN IMPRINT OF HAL LEONARD LLC

Published in 2017 by Applause Theatre & Cinema Books
An Imprint of Hal Leonard LLC
7777 West Bluemound Road
Milwaukee, WI 53213

Trade Book Division Editorial Offices
33 Plymouth St., Montclair, NJ 07042

Printed in the United States of America

Book design by Lynn Bergesen, UB Communications

Library of Congress Cataloging-in-Publication Data

Names: Kellerman, Lira editor.
Title: Break the rules and get the part : thirty monologues for women / Lira
    Kellerman [editor].
Description: Milwaukee, WI : Applause Theatre & Cinema Books, 2017.
Identifiers: LCCN 2016052125 | ISBN 9781495075414 (pbk.)
Subjects: LCSH: Monologues. | Acting—Auditions.
Classification: LCC PN2080 .B75 2017 | DDC 808.82/45—dc23
LC record available at https://lccn.loc.gov/2016052125

www.applausebooks.com

For Anthony

Everything, always, for you.

Io ti amo, con tutto il cuore, per sempre.

E si non ti piace, dolce mio, va dunatila en culo.

"The foolish and wicked practice of profane cursing and swearing is a vice so mean and low that every person of sense and character detests and despises it."

—George Washington

◇◇◇◇◇◇◇◇◇◇◇◇◇◇◇◇◇

Contents

◇◇◇◇◇◇◇◇◇◇◇◇◇◇◇◇◇◇◇

Preface

I used to hate monologues. They just seemed like endless words strung together to talk about nothing. They're hard to find, they're hard to do, but search for and perform them we must; it's always going to be part of the audition process until we don't have to audition anymore.

There's so much potential in monologue books. We open them, skim them, hoping to find something that speaks to us, and if a book has just two pieces we can use, we consider it a success and hope the other monologues might fit us later on down the road. Sometimes they do. Most of the time, however, they don't.

I was sick of monologues that didn't have a story; that had no meat, no conflict, no humor, no drama. Sure, my humor and drama is different from your humor and drama, but monologues need to have a point, don't they? We're not auditioning just to show off our memorization skills, are we?

So, yeah, I used to hate them. They never felt like they had *enough* for me. Until I started breaking rules. And I'm going to show you how to break the rules, too. How to go against the rules you were taught. How to break away from ideas that aren't helpful. How to take a piece and truly make it your own.

The most helpful part of this book, however, is that you can take these broken rules and apply them to *other* books and monologues *you already have*. After you finish this, after you read the entire thing from beginning to end, I want you to find all the other pieces in your repertoire, the other monologues in your other books, and see how you can make them timely, how you can make them better, but, most importantly, how you can make them *your own*.

What Is a Monologue?

I'm so glad you asked. A monologue is an unnaturally long speech by a character dominating a conversation. They're often performed as audition pieces where you stand in a room and talk to the other character who isn't there with you. Instead of feeding off another actor's energy and body language, you're feeding off a blank wall. It's incredibly weird and awkward. Most actors would rather cold read and perform material they've never seen before than perform a monologue, and for good reason: monologues are hard.

Playwrights wrote these long speeches to showcase their dramatic writing, but read a play written in the last few years, and you'll read text that could also feel right at home on your television. Dialogue is more back-and-forth these days, more conversational, and you'll be hard-pressed to find characters speaking in lengthy paragraphs to one another anymore because of how utterly unnatural it is. Think about the last conversation you had. You were probably interrupting and being interrupted, expounding on one tangent after another, and then going back to the original point. Natural dialogue on the page sounds like natural dialogue in real life, and this natural-sounding trend continues on.

Unfortunately, there is absolutely nothing natural about mono-logues, which is probably why many of us hate doing them. Whether you're a new actor or a seasoned one, finding good monologues that speak to you, that have the comedic or dramatic beats you need, that have great emotional arcs, takes *forever*. You'll pick several that are just okay, and you'll perform them just okay because there are no meaty parts to sink your teeth into. This book is different: packed with filet mignon-ologues, designed intentionally with relatable themes in mind for women at different ages. These monologues were written specifically so that you could find the emotional beats, work the arc, and have a one-minute play that shows *you* off. And, if you're vegetarian, don't worry, the meat was just a pun. So, meat eaters, vegetarians, vegans, gluten free: Let's. Do. This.

Why This Book?

Acting is your passion; you're a storyteller and you can't imagine doing anything else. You are learning monologues, reading acting books, studying movies, and doing everything you can to be the best actor out there. An actor who knows when to apply what rules to which character for which style for which medium.

If you've been performing monologues at auditions and aren't booking roles, let's face it: something is not working and it's probably you. You're following archaic rules that just don't work anymore. Acting has changed dramatically in the last fifty years. Check out any black-and-white classic from your library or online streaming service, and compare it to the films currently in movie theaters; words are over-enunciated and everything seems overplayed. The rules taught for performing today's monologues are from decades-old acting styles and acting coaches who've been dead for years.

I am going to assume that you're also in an acting class of some sort. If your goal is to also be a film and television actor, and you're in a major filming hub like Los Angeles, New York, or Atlanta, get in a reputable on-camera class now. Not only are you going to meet amazing people who will become close friends, but you'll learn how to adapt your craft, getting smaller and smaller to fit that medium. The cinematic world is forever changing, and if you're not changing with it, you're not getting your chance to act.

I want you to have your chance. I want you to showcase the phenomenal actor inside you. If old rules and bad monologues are trapping her, let's break down the barriers, break the rules, and Get. You. That. Part!

Helpful Direction

Sometimes a little direction is needed to take a monologue from good to great. A little nudge might be all you need, and if you don't want to use it, you don't have to. Sometimes it's just a little easier to understand a monologue from a monologue book when the writer offers an idea on how to perform it. You don't get backstory, plot, or relationships in a monologue book like you would in a play, so an author's point of view or direction could be helpful to you until you learn how to self-direct and to build characters on your own. As with all acting advice, however, use what works and throw the rest out. You are by no means obligated to use any Helpful Direction offered in this book, but I sure do recommend it!

I also strongly recommend reading each and every monologue and its Helpful Direction straight through like a normal book. This way, you'll come across Helpful Directions mentioned in one piece that can easily apply to another one. Reading thirty monologues with suggestions and ideas on how to perform them will help you hone your self-directing skills so that you can go back to your other monologue books and find (or deliberately insert!) meaty emotional arcs, just by applying what you've learned from this book.

Finding a Good Monologue

How do you find a good monologue? By making sure that comedic monologues have funny bits to play while continually building the stakes and tension, and that dramatic monologues have an arc where the character has an emotional revelation. Seriocomic monologues touch on both, with a joke or two here, and a definite emotional hiccup there. If monologues don't have these qualities, they're boring, which makes you, the actor, boring. Auditors don't need to see any more of a boring actor, as your headshot will have already been placed in the "no" pile.

Oh, the Pressure!

Your armpits are sweaty, your hands are shaking, and you stand before a panel of judges who have been critiquing everything about you since you entered the room. And now they have the bizarre task of evaluating how you talk to thin air.

If it's a serious monologue, you've walked into the audition space, made pleasant small talk about your day, and then been forced to switch to on-the-verge crying at the top of your piece. Even though they say, "Whenever you're ready," you are wasting their time if you take more than ten seconds. You feel it, they feel it. They continue to stare at you, waiting, and when you begin, all you think about is them assessing you. You're inside your head and wondering if you're performing well because your scene partner, whom you would normally be focusing on and reacting to, isn't really there. Oh, crap, are your eyes not watering at the part where you say your eyes are watering? There's. So. Much. Pressure!

How can you alleviate most of the pressure before it even begins? By being fully connected to the piece you're about to perform by *loving* your piece. By finding the things you can *personalize* to make it yours. By *changing* what you need to change to show off your incredible skills. This book is filled with original monologues the auditors have never heard before, and, best of all, they are all going to be catered to *you* because their whole point is to show *you* off.

What Do Auditors Even Want to See?

Auditors need to see a full, complex story told in less than a minute. How do we do that? With emotional arcs, or *emotional 180s*. Look at the end of the monologue that catches your fancy. Is your character crying at the end? Then she might be happy at the beginning! Is she starting off angry? Then maybe she's laughing at the end. Not all monologues have emotional 180s at their start and finish, however. Some have them in the middle, so you might be sad in the beginning and end, but making jokes in between.

But yes, *show the emotional arc*. Take us on that journey. Make us care! The only reason we watch anyone on stage, on film, on television is to care about what they've been through, what they're going through, and what's going to happen to them next. Make us care and we will want to see more of you. Every time.

There Are Rules
Made to Be Broken!

How many times have you performed a monologue only to leave the room kicking yourself for not getting to where you needed to be emotionally? How many times have you thought you've done well, only to not even get a callback? How many hours have you wasted trying to find the perfect monologue, only to discover that none really fit you, are long enough, short enough, or have the heightened emotion you need to show off your talent?

Everything you've ever learned about performing monologues isn't necessarily the best way to show off *you*, the actor. Yes, you have to know the rules to break them, but *it is absolutely okay* to break these rules. Acting is always about choices, so make the choice that is going to get you the part.

Break the Rules!

That's right, break them! The biggest secret I can tell you, the auditioning actor, is that the most important thing about the monologue isn't the writing, it's *you*, the actor performing it. Read the following tips and advice and see which rules you can break to benefit you and your audition. You really can get the part by breaking the rules.

Break the Rule:
Be Professional

You've been taught that you must absolutely be professional when you walk into a casting office or audition space. Shoulders back, chest out, only speaking when spoken to, etc.

Unfortunately, that comes across as haughty and snobbish, and you carry an air about you that suggests you don't even want to be there. That's exactly the person your auditors don't want to work with. Instead, treat it like a third date and walk into the room as yourself! If you crack jokes, crack jokes! Be friendly! Be you! Your auditors will make small talk to try and get a sense of who you are as a person, so be the very best person you can be: yourself. You've got this!

◇◇◇◇◇◇

Break the Rule:
You Must Introduce
Your Monologue

Unless you're auditioning to get into a school and they've stated that you must introduce your monologue, don't bother, because, quite honestly, no one cares. Just take the time you would have spent introducing it to get into character instead, giving you several more seconds to focus yourself, take a breath, and get ready to tell your story. If your auditors care where it's from, they'll ask you when you're done! And they'll get the relaxed version of you and the story of how you found it, instead of a nervous actor woodenly reciting the name of it as she's simultaneously mentally preparing to perform it.

If they liked your performance, and they liked you, they might even ask about your process, and they'll find you charming, calm, and professional as you describe it, all because you broke this one simple rule.

◇◇◇◇◇◇

Break the Rule:
Your Monologue Must Be
from a Published Play

Oh, it *must* be from a published play? Bullshit.

Sometimes you'll be asked to perform a monologue from a play because the auditors want to see you perform a piece that has a fully built character with a full plot, subplot, arcs, the whole shebang. The truth is, they really don't care where it's from unless they specifically requested a Shakespearean monologue or other classical work.

What do you do if they insist that your audition piece be from a published play, but your favorite monologue is from this book?

◇◇◇◇◇◇

Improvise. Make up a title! Make up a name for the playwright! I have done this very thing and the casting director pretended he had heard of the play I made up on the spot. Casting will have seen the same five monologues over and over again and this one will be a huge breath of fresh air. *They absolutely will not care where it's from as long as you perform it well.* Their sole purpose is to find great talent. Once they do, once they find *you*, nothing else matters.

◇◇◇◇◇◇

Break the Rule:
You Must Look at Someone
When Performing

Never, ever direct your monologue at your auditors, because you'll be making them your unwilling scene partner. Their job right now is to assess your acting skills! Don't distract them by forcing them to act with you.

If you're in a small theater, pick a chair in one of the last rows, and if you're in a huge theater, find a theater seat a few spots to the right or left of your auditors. In a small casting office or room? Pick a spot about a foot above their heads and perform to that spot. It's easier if you make the spot something memorable, like the left corner of the picture frame on the wall, or the plant on the top of the bookshelf. It's easier to look at actual things than a blank circle on the white wall. When I audition in a dance space with mirrors, I love to look at myself because I can react to myself, and I happen to think I'm an excellent scene partner!

Also, do not stare down your spot or chair the whole time. You don't stare into someone's eyes for the entire duration of a real-life conversation; you look at the floor, you look away, and when you need to drive a point home, you look back into their eyes. *Always*

◇◇◇◇◇◇

pay attention to how you talk to people in real life. Actors are always studying humans and how we react to them in all situations. What's true to life is also true on stage.

If you address more than one person in your monologue, make sure you place these imaginary people a few feet apart. When you look back and forth between them, it will be easy to tell you are speaking to two different people. It's just a small technical thing that adds a wonderful dimension to your performance.

∞∞∞∞∞

Break the Rule:
You Must Block Your Monologue

For a dramatic monologue, you don't really need to move. You don't have to stay glued to your spot, per se, and if you feel the impulse to take a step forward, go for it, but for the most part, you can stay exactly where you are.

Always stay back at least six feet away from those auditioning you. The more space, the better. If you're on a stage and they're in the audience, great. If you're in a cramped office, make sure you're not in their immediate personal space. If you have practiced your monologue standing up (good for you!) and there's a chair in your way, move the chair. You don't even have to ask! You just say, "I'm going to move this chair," commanding the space, and they'll immediately see you as a seasoned performer.

Always stand if you can. For comedic monologues your gestures will be bigger, your emotions heightened, and you can move a few steps if the piece demands it. Just adjust the amount you move to the amount of space you have. If you notice a camera and are being taped, it's fine to ask if the camera operator will follow you. If the camera is stationary, ask what your frame is and adjust to that. If they are shooting from your belly button up, you need to tighten everything and use your normal, inside voice. You don't shout in a library, and you don't project in a casting office.

Use your phone to record yourself performing your monologue. Is it something that looks like it could be on television, or do you need to adjust and make everything smaller? You can even upload the video onto your social networking sites and have your actor friends critique you.

Also, be prepared to perform your monologue on a gigantic stage as well as in a small corridor with people walking by. I've done both and everything in between. You will, too.

◇◇◇◇◇◇

Break the Rule: You Must Serve the Text

You have been told this over and over and over and over again: Be true to the intentions of the playwright. Serve the Text. You know what? *Fuck the Text.* I cannot stress this enough. You did not memorize all those lines for your audition to show that the playwright could string together a bunch of sentences. No. You're speaking the speech to show off how great an actor you are. *Serve the text in a play, but in an audition, let the text serve you!* Change what you need in order to succeed! For example, I once used a monologue from a play written in the eighties that referenced eighties movies to make a point. It was topical in its own decade, but now the monologue was terribly dated. So, instead of using the films in the text, I went online, read their summaries, and replaced them with similarly themed films that were currently playing at movie theaters. By Fucking the Text, I transformed a horribly dated monologue into one that was current and closer to what the playwright originally intended! *Be a smart actor to be a better actor.*

If your monologue is too long, cut it! Cut out parts you don't like! Your monologue only needs to be one minute, because anyone can tell how good an actor you are in the first five seconds; the next fifty-five are just a courtesy.

Anytime you are working a monologue and the character refers to someone, you have to know what your relationship to that person is. If you're talking about Bella, who is she? Do you like her? Do you hate her guts? What if she's your sister and you're talking about how much you miss her? Let's say your real sister's name is Vanessa, and you do miss her very much. Why not change Bella to Vanessa?

If you are working a monologue where you are going on about how much you hate your father, but your relationship with your dad is actually pretty stellar, substitute a person you do hate, like your lousy, cheating ex. Simple, small things like changing the names and the relationships will help naturally stir up your emotions, connecting you to the piece.

Also, why not change the age? The gender? If it's a monologue where the character is breaking up with her boyfriend, but you want it to be a character breaking up with her wife, Fuck the Text, change the boyfriend's gender, and change all the pronouns! If she mentions they fought in health class, change it to the wine store! Once you decide to perform a particular monologue from a monologue book, it is no longer that author's monologue, it is yours. Change it. Rewrite it. Take control of what you want to showcase by showcasing what you can control: the monologue.

◇◇◇◇◇◇

Break the Rule:
You Mustn't Include Vocalized Pauses

When most people talk, they use the words "um," "uh," and "like," so much that they don't even hear them anymore. These are called vocalized pauses, and you've probably been drilled to get rid of them if you studied theater. Vocalized pauses, however, can color your monologue into a verbal masterpiece. If you can sprinkle them in and it's natural, great. If you sprinkle them in and it sounds weird to the point of giving the impression that you can't remember the next word, lose them. But, like, seriously, the younger you are, the more, like, forgiving people will be! It could make the monologue for a woman in her forties sound like it was written for a girl going on seventeen.

Also good for changing the age of a really great monologue? Swear words. If you find a great piece written for a character younger than you filled with a bunch of cusses, take them out. Found a great piece for someone older than you? Yup, throw in a few ums and likes, and toss in some swears. And while we're on the subject, swear words are never meant to be emphasized; it's the word *after* them that should be stressed. Swear words are filler to give the next word more weight. For example, if your character says "He's so fucking cruel," *cruel* is the word that needs your love and attention. Don't believe me? Watch for it in real-life conversations. I fucking swear it's true.

∽∽∽∽∽∽

Break the Rule:
You Must Build Your Character
from Scratch

I remember taking a Building a Character class and having to write a five-page biography about my character: her childhood, schooling, socioeconomic class, status, hobbies, spending habits, parenting style, dental history, and, oh my God, seriously? Did my professor even read the busywork she'd assigned us? No. And it could have been so much easier if I had just gone ahead and thought, who is this character *like*?

Does your character remind you of someone you can pull some real-life quirks from? Sketch performers base many of their characters and quirks on real people they've seen, watched, met, or known. Johnny Depp famously used his friend Keith Richards as inspiration for his character Captain Jack Sparrow in *Pirates of the Caribbean*, and Seth MacFarlane based his *Family Guy* character voice for Peter Griffin on a security guard he knew while in college. Use your fun best friend Sarah to inspire quirks and personality traits. Use Uncle Bob's odd tics to establish an introverted type. Pull from anyone and everyone you know.

Also, what about *you*? How would you act in the given circumstances in your monologue? You yourself might be exactly the character your auditors are looking for.

◇◇◇◇◇◇

Break the Rule: Women Must Only Perform Monologues for Women

Lots of plays are written by men, and, since most storytellers use grains of truth from their own experiences, you'll read a lot of plays about men featuring male problems with small female characters whose sole purpose is to teach a major life lesson to the male lead. The underwritten female characters have a few lines here or there while the male leads have great monologues. So why not use the great monologues?

Monologues written for men aren't always gender-specific, so, if you can find one you like, use it. No one says you can't. Change a few pronouns and you're safe. Most monologues for women seem flippant or stupid, nothing suitable for showing off. Don't let a small thing like not having a penis make you suffer through lesser monologues. With institutional, cultural, and social sexism, we're already suffering enough!

Break the Barrier

If you haven't yet earned your Bachelor of Fine Arts in Theater, with a Concentration in Performing on the Stage, or if you don't plan to, allow me to define some acting terms. Knowing and understanding the terms enables you to apply them to your work, making you a better performer. It also makes you easier to direct, should your auditors ask you to perform your monologue again, but with some adjustments. And let me be clear: You absolutely could have killed it and wowed them with your acting performance, but they'll just about always give you notes or direction to see if you can understand and take their directing style, and if you're someone they could easily work with.

Objective

You have to know not only what you're saying in your monologue, but also why you're saying it. Your *objective* is what you want from the other person, and how you define your objective will give your lines purpose. Everything you do and say is because you want something.

For instance, let's take a look at the sentence "I never thought you'd do something like that." You could say that line a variety of ways, depending on what you want from the other person. If you want to feel superior to them, and want to make them feel bad, you would say that line in a manner calculated to shame them. If you want them to like you, you might say that line flirtatiously.

A monologue could have several objectives in it. If you want to make the other character feel bad and say something hurtful to them in the monologue, your objective immediately after that might be to try to make them like you again, so you'd say your next line apologetically. A lot of it will depend on your relationship with the person you're speaking to.

Relationship

The way you say things will be determined not only by what you want from the other person, but also by your *relationship* with them. Take the line "Okay." It's just one word, but it can say so much! Let's say you're fourteen, it's winter break, and your mom just assigned you yet another chore. That one word might be dragged out to show your annoyance. Let's say you're in your twenties and your hot crush just asked if you wanted to go grab a drink after work. Now that one word is going to be flirtatious and happy and upbeat. Let's say you're in your thirties and you're super unhappy with the amount of work you've been given at your job, but your boss asks you if you can take on one more assignment. You don't want to be fired, so that one word will sound dramatically different from the previous two examples.

Relationship is everything. It will dictate how you define your objectives and what tactics you'll use to reach your goals, so it is extremely important to know specifically to whom you're speaking in your monologue, and how you feel about that person at all times in your piece.

Tactics

You can't always get what you want, and as soon as you understand that, you switch *tactics*. You change your actions or strategy to help you achieve your objective, and you've been doing this ever since you were a small child.

Let's say, for instance, you're four years old and really want ice cream for dinner. Your objective is to eat ice cream. You ask your mom if you can have ice cream for dinner. She responds that you cannot. You did not achieve your objective, so you change your tactic. Now you tack on "Pretty please?" to your request. You are denied again. Dang it! You really want ice cream! You switch tactics.

Now you bargain and say, "If you give me ice cream for dinner, I'll clean my room." Denied again. You still need to hit your objective, so you change tactics once more. Now you threaten your poor mother and say, "If you don't give me ice cream for dinner, I'll hold my breath until I die!" Your mom loves you, but she also understands how the human body works and knows you'll simply pass out first. She again says you can't have ice cream. But that ice cream, though! It's so good! You still haven't hit your objective, so you change tactics again. You throw yourself on the floor and scream your head off until you see her open the freezer and scoop out some ice cream so that you'll shut up. Success!

The entire above scene not only has everything you need in a monologue, but also everything you need in a good story: objective, tactics, an escalation, a climax, and a resolution!

Having clear tactic changes in your monologues shows a deep understanding of dramatic story and text.

Beats

A *beat* is a decision, discovery, or reaction that alters the way you behave in your piece to get what you want, and is usually represented by a pause or change in tactics or emotion. Beats help your monologue go from a long, drab story to a mini-play filled with human drama that rivets your audience.

Let's go back to four-year-old you and the ice cream. You've just asked if you can have ice cream for dinner, and your mom has responded that you cannot. You take a beat—in this case, a small pause while you think what to do next. You look at the floor, and then you think to yourself, "Oh! The magic word!" You've discovered a new way to get ice cream! You look back up to your mother and ask, "Pretty please, can I have ice cream for dinner?" You are hopeful, sincere. She says no. Beat change! You're not happy; you're angry now! You're reacting to her keeping you from your objective. In this particular story, there are several beat changes, and there are several beat changes in monologues, too. Always search for them. You must find them. Sometimes you may even feel like you have to force one in. That's okay. They will always make your performance better.

Subtext

Sometimes we say something when we actually mean something else. In fact, when we're communicating with others, we do it a lot. *Subtext* is the invisible text just below the actual text that colors what you're saying and why. For instance, let's say you have a coworker who completely messed up his task. You might say, "That's not how you're supposed to do it." With that sentence, you could easily show him with subtext either that you think he's a complete idiot, he's wasting everyone's time, and you wish you could fire him, or that you are here to help him, and you have a crush on him.

Seemingly normal, boring lines could be made painfully beautiful just by finding the subtext to what your character is saying. Sometimes it's obvious, sometimes you have to force it in to make the piece more interesting, but your performance will always be better because you understand what this is and know when and how to use it.

Environment

Your character's *environment* is going to dictate how she speaks to the other person in the monologue, and you can always use that to your acting advantage! Let's use a real-life example to show what I mean. Let's say you're fighting with your significant other in a movie theater. You're not going to be yelling at one another; you're going to be using hushed voices, trying not to disturb the other patrons. If a monologue took place in the same movie theater environment, you'd deliver it in the same way. You might even add an "Oh, 'shh' yourself!" to an invisible person to your right or left to show that you're bothering the other people in the theater with you. Small things like that in the monologue can really color your work and make it real. *Always* consider where you are in your piece and how that affects your dialogue and actions. If it's never mentioned where you are, pick an interesting place and commit to it, reacting as you would if you were really saying those words in that specific place.

Moments Before and After

There is an art to pretending that puts your headshot and résumé ahead of the rest; if you can act before and after your monologue, you have a complete story with a beginning, middle, and end that keeps us engaged and wanting more. Let's say you have a monologue and you make the choice to set the piece in an elevator. Instead of just forging ahead with the memorized words, create a *moment before* in your environment. What would you do if you really were in an elevator? Why, you'd hit a button, take a small step back, and stand and watch the elevator numbers at the top of the doors change. You do this for a quick beat before you start your monologue, and wow! Utter brilliance! You established your environment in your moment before, and we really believed you were in an elevator! Brava! Moments before immediately show that you know what you're doing.

There is also the *moment after*. Many new actors will finish reciting their lines and then look immediately relieved for having gotten every word right. Or they'll look pained because they forgot a chunk or switched a sentence around. An inexperienced actor might even say, "Scene," to indicate that the monologue is finished. It's nerves, it's fear, and it robs the auditors of a great ending. It's like the auditors were having the most wonderful, luxurious yawn, and then the actor punched them in the face.

Giving an extra beat after you finish your monologue shows us you understand drama. When you finish talking, you're not finished acting! Allow your invisible scene partner to react to what you just said. And (here's where magic happens!) react to *that*.

For example, I once had a monologue that ended with the question "Did you ever love me?" The first few times I performed it, I waited in anticipation of what my invisible partner was going to say, but quickly realized that if my invisible scene partner gave me the clear impression that in fact he had never loved me, my monologue wasn't over! I now had an extra seven brilliant seconds in which to be completely torn apart. My lines were done, but my monologue still had another few silent beats to it. Rainbows and unicorns swirled around me because the auditors were riveted. I was acting more in that moment after and being truer to real life in that moment simply because I asked myself, "What would happen in my moment after if I heard him say 'No'?" Moments after can transform a pretty good actor into a phenomenal one.

Inner Monologue

Just as you are constantly thinking when you're listening and even when you're talking, so is your character. Her *inner monologue* is what she's thinking about while she's speaking and helps steer the piece into something very real and relatable.

Let's say your character is talking about an abusive ex-lover, and she says, "He hit me." How does your interpretation of that line change if in your head, as your character, your inner monologue has you repeating over and over again that he hit you because you deserved it? What does that do to a character? How does feeling she deserved to be beaten color the rest of her words?

What if you are playing a character who is screaming that she doesn't need her mother's help? If your line is, "Leave me alone!"

how does your interpretation of it change if your character's inner monologue is that she actually needs her mother to stay? How does that inner monologue drive your moment after if your mother does leave? How are you showing the audience the agony of having pushed her away when you absolutely needed her the most?

An inner monologue can add incredible layers and depth to what might at first glance appear to be a superficial story.

Break a Leg!

Like I said, finding a good monologue is extremely hard, but I do believe you've got a good thirty awaiting your take, your interpretation, and your own personal essence. These are all little stories, and you, my friend, are not just an actor, but a *storyteller*. Take me on your emotional journey with you. Make me want to hear more from you. Make me want no one else but you. Make me cast you.

You can do it.

I believe in you.

<><><><><><><><><><><><><><><><><><><><><><><><><><><><><><><><><><><><><><>

DRAMATIC MONOLOGUES

◇◇◇◇◇◇

Monologue 1

Stay positive? I'm sick of it. I can't do this anymore. This is not going to end the happy way everyone says it will. They keep telling me chin up, smile, laugh. I don't want to laugh. I can't laugh. He's thinner and weaker. He can't even tell me he loves me anymore. Be positive, they all say. I am positive. I am positive he is going to die.

◇◇◇◇◇◇

◇◇◇◇◇◇◇

Helpful Direction

Take your time with this one! It's only twelve sentences, but the power lies within your delivery. This might look boring at first, but if someone told you to "Stay positive!" for the twentieth time in two hours while your husband/boyfriend/brother (or Fuck the Text: your girlfriend/wife/mother/sister) was dying, you might just flip out on them at this point. Play with the punctuation, exchanging periods for exclamation points if you want to. Also, try repeating a line that really resonates with you. Repeating certain sentences, and highlighting different words within them, might help you trigger the emotions you need for this monologue to truly shine. For instance, you might say, "I can't *do* this anymore," and, repeating it, stress a different word, like, "I can't do this *anymore!*"

Really have a hard time with finally confiding that he can't tell her he loves her anymore. Is this the first time she's telling anyone this? If it breaks your heart, it's breaking your auditor's.

The last three sentences . . . oy vey. She could start laughing when she says, "I am positive." She could be making a sad joke to cope. Play around and see if she continues to laugh, or if she's crying and overcome with grief. The most important thing in this piece is to have more than just one emotion. Different levels are going to show you can dig deep into something "sad" and make it just as absurdly complicated as real life.

◇◇◇◇◇◇◇

◇◇◇◇◇◇

Monologue 2

As soon as we found out, we called everyone we knew. There was so much happy squealing. Brandon even organized a last-minute get together where we all drank sparkling cider and picked out the most atrocious names we could think of. When I lost it . . . I couldn't get out of bed. People were still calling, congratulating, offering their favorite name ideas, while my body was cramping and bleeding, expelling the baby I couldn't keep alive. One minute I was picking out pastel paint, the next . . . Brandon keeps asking me if I'm okay. I'm not okay.

◇◇◇◇◇◇

◇◇◇◇◇◇◇

Helpful Direction

When you're talking about the happy moments, be happy! This is great! And then, wham! No one is expecting this monologue to be as sad as it is when you start on a high note, and it definitely gives the beat change and emotional arc more weight.

Use the ellipses to figure out if you want to actually say what's next. Perhaps, during that silent beat, your inner monologue tells you it's too much, so you shift gears by switching topics. This poor character is trying to keep everything together, but it's still too new, too raw, and she's still hurting.

Also, the last line—how does she say it? Is she crying? Or does she say it after trying to clean herself up and be "normal" again? How else could she say it? Try it all the ways.

◇◇◇◇◇◇◇

◇◇◇◇◇◇

Monologue 3

When you were pregnant with your last one, did you ever . . . you know, think what life would've been like had you never gotten married so young? I wonder what life would've been like if me and Randy never got together. Whether I'd be some famous model in New York or some such. Free, you know? Not tied down to chores and responsibilities. I could just up and go wherever and whenever I wanted. Sounds neat, don't it? I think about it and then I feel guilty, 'cause I want to be a good mama. I do. I just don't know if I was ready for all this, like I thought I was, you know? It all sounded so easy, and everyone was so excited when I told them I was pregnant. Everyone was nice as pie, too. But now . . . I'm just so tired. Tired all the time. I haven't been myself in weeks. Almost makes me wish I was a hamster just so I could eat one of the twins and lighten my load.

◇◇◇◇◇◇

◇◇◇◇◇◇◇

Helpful Direction

This girl is emotionally exhausted, and she knows she'll never see her dreams realized. There's so much quiet sadness in that.

Maybe this girl's mother and grandmother and great-grandmother were all married and pregnant at eighteen, and this girl said, "No, I'm going to go and be somebody in the big city!" and then fell prey to the same lifestyle she swore she wouldn't. Then she's probably fighting with the duality of loving her children and wishing she'd never had them, a conflict people don't share readily.

So who is she talking to? Her best friend? Her aunt? She's wistful, but she's also lifting a huge burden of guilt off her shoulders by finally talking about it. Find where she's scared to talk about it and then relieved. Is her last line a joke to ease the tension? Is she absolutely serious about it? How does the person she's speaking to react to what she's saying, and how does your character react to that? There are many levels to play.

◇◇◇◇◇◇◇

◇◇◇◇◇◇

Monologue 4

She was born two and a half months early. She was so tiny. Tiny little fingers, teeny, tiny toes. Yellow skin from jaundice. She was so underdeveloped, so weak. Babies are born fat, happy. She was born skinny, scared. Sometimes, she would forget to breathe, and then her heart rate would dip all over again. Apneas and bradycardias. I didn't even want to name her because I knew God was only letting me borrow her for a few days, just to let me see what being a mom was like. I was a mom, a good mom, for three days, five hours, and four minutes.

◇◇◇◇◇◇

◇◇◇◇◇◇◇

Helpful Direction

It is especially important to research and see what a twenty-six-week-old fetus looks like so you can get an idea of just how scared this character is. And what environment are you putting her in? Where is she? A grieving mothers' support group? Prison? Her kitchen? How does her environment add to her character and the way she says her words in this piece?

Backstory is especially helpful here. Who is she? How old is she? Is this her first baby at twenty-two? Is this her last chance for one at forty-two? How much did she want this baby? Take your time with the beats.

How are you creating her emotional arc? Where are her emotional 180s in the piece? Does she smile? Laugh? Where in this piece is she happy?

And if you feel the impulse at the end to repeat, "A very good mom, a very good mom," to help you get to the emotions you want, Fuck the Text and do it.

◇◇◇◇◇◇◇

◇◇◇◇◇◇

Monologue 5

Where have you been? Seriously, where have you been? I called, I texted, nothing. The first day went by, fine, no big deal, I know you work long hours, but a second day goes by? A third? And I'm by myself going through this thing, and I can't get ahold of you. Do you know how scary this whole thing has been for me? Do you know how isolated I am? How lonely? And I swear to God, you do this every time you start seeing someone new. I get it, I really do, he's interesting, and it's brand-new and exciting, but you can't keep on forgetting about me. Where were you? I'm all by myself and I needed you, but you weren't there. You weren't there. On purpose. Why?

◇◇◇◇◇◇

◇◇◇◇◇◇

Helpful Direction

Up. The. Stakes. The first question you must ask yourself is what is this "thing" the character is talking about? If she cut her finger, the stakes are low. If she needed her friend to drive her to her abortion and she flaked, the stakes are high. The higher the stakes, the higher your emotional response. Have you gone through a difficult situation where you felt abandoned? Use it. Make that your thing.

And who is she talking to? Her best friend, her mother, her brother, her ex? Let that color your response.

Also, think about levels. There are parts where she's incredulous, accusatory, and then there's a small bit of understanding. Find the emotional 180s and play around with them. How many different emotions can you play within this piece?

She also repeats herself. Anytime you repeat yourself, you must highlight different words on the repetition.

The last word of the piece gives you a beautiful moment after, where you can react to what the other person says. What difference does it make to your moment after if you imagine the other person says, "I'm sorry, I should have been there," versus, "You did this to yourself and I don't care"? Play with what works best for you.

◇◇◇◇◇◇

◇◇◇◇◇◇

Monologue 6

It's genetic! Don't you understand? What's happening to her is going to happen to me! Do you know how terrifying that is? People are going to leave me because they won't know what to do with me; they won't know how to take care of me. I am going to have the same problems, need the same medication, and want to die but be kept alive for no good reason, just like she is. I am so afraid. I am checking for symptoms every day. Can you blame me? I am my mother's daughter in every way. You have two choices here. Either understand and help me get through this, or give up on me and leave. Just like my father did.

◇◇◇◇◇◇

◇◇◇◇◇◇◇

Helpful Direction

Okay. Your voice is raised at the very beginning, which means that you're going to have to center your voice and emotions at the middle and then rise a bit again at the end. You're a vocal roller coaster, not a constant scream. Screams are exhausting to listen to, and if you scream and yell for the entirety of any monologue, you'll immediately be thrown into the "no" pile because you've immediately made it clear you can't find your emotional 180s.

Now consider your environment. Is she in a hospital? Is she aware of other people listening? You can start your monologue intensely, then, after the first two sentences, take a beat to look around at your surroundings to show that your character is aware others can hear her. She can be embarrassed by that and adjust her volume accordingly.

I also love the line "I am so afraid." How are you playing it? Are you crying? What if you're laughing? Where can you play the emotional 180s to make this piece, and therefore *you*, more interesting?

There are lots of fun ways to do this.

◇◇◇◇◇◇◇

∞∞∞∞∞∞

Monologue 7

Sometimes I swear he's right next to me. When I'm drawing my next breath, I can almost hear him do the same. Sometimes he's gently patting my knee, like he used to when we'd be sitting next each other and I said something funny. Sometimes I swear he's just in the next room, waiting patiently while I'm taking too long to get ready. . . . When I found him, curled up in all that pain . . . I was paralyzed. I couldn't move to help him. And I know he could've lived if I had only gotten to him in time.

∞∞∞∞∞∞

◇◇◇◇◇◇◇

Helpful Direction

This character has to believe that her husband/father/Fuck the Text is somehow really comforting her when she still feels so terribly guilty for his death. She must be devastated, and to go from happy/wistful to guilty/sad is a beautiful transition, so definitely find your emotional 180s.

How did you find him? Was it a heart attack? Suicide? When you say you found him, know exactly in what way, and picture it, see it, feel it, as you're performing this piece. It's simple, but so strong.

And for this piece, because the drama is small, it's okay to sit in a chair if one is available. One caveat: because these emotions are intense, you might find yourself naturally faced toward the floor. Make a note if you're doing that while you're rehearsing this piece, and always make sure your face is out so your audience can see you. You really don't want them to miss a thing here.

◇◇◇◇◇◇◇

∞∞∞∞∞

Monologue 8

Do you see this? This tiny white pill? This is calmness. This is inner peace. This is sanity. This is everything I'm not and can't have unless I swallow it. This tiny white pill is the exact reason why you won't love me. Isn't it tragic? Because once I am perfectly balanced, I'll decide that I don't really need any of it. So the tiny white pills in the small orange bottle—I'll stop taking them. And I'll be fine. For a day or two. But you will notice that I'm acting a little different. Maybe it's the time of the month for me. You won't know. But you're invested in me now. I'll become strange. And stranger. And the tiny white pills that I've flushed down the toilet, they're never coming back. And suddenly you're going to realize that you don't want to deal with me and my idiosyncrasies, my drama. But you know what? I'm going to cut you off at the pass. Because I know how it's all going to play out, and I'm sick of it. I love you. So I'm letting you go. I'm not even giving you a choice. It's over. Over! Do you hear me!? Get out! Get out! Leave!

∞∞∞∞∞

◇◇◇◇◇◇◇

Helpful Direction

How manic is this character? How bipolar is she? How often is she calculating, intimidating, and being vulnerable? Is it every other sentence? More often? Less? Is there no pattern to her craziness? Do you switch it up depending on your own mood? Awesome! If you ever want to have a piece to showcase how you can manipulate and taunt, flirt and pull away, stay grounded and fly off the handle, this is it. Just don't forget to empathize, because she does want to love and be loved but she's terrified of it.

Consider when you're addressing the other person, and when you're looking at the pill. The back-and-forth between the two will make you very interesting. Go ahead and use a mint from your purse for a prop. Don't have one? Easily fake it by rubbing your forefinger on your thumb.

What happens after the last sentence? Does the other person leave? Stay? Which emotion is she going through when she hears a response in the moment after? That's how you leave us wanting more.

◇◇◇◇◇◇◇

◇◇◇◇◇◇

Monologue 9

When I woke up, I couldn't feel my legs. The windshield was cracked where I had hit it. Linda was in the passenger seat, her body flopped against mine. The windshield in front of her was a cobweb splattered with her blood. There was so much of it. I remember staring at it, focusing on how perfectly deep a red it was. I blinked white flashes and could only hear a high-pitched whine, nothing else. I knew I was in shock. So I kept concentrating on the blood. How red, God, the most beautiful shade of red. I put my hand on Linda's leg next to mine. Maybe if she could feel me, she wouldn't be as scared as I was when she woke up. But she never woke up. She died next to me. I was seventeen. I was driving.

◇◇◇◇◇◇

◇◇◇◇◇◇◇

Helpful Direction

She killed her sister/best friend/mom/daughter/granddaughter/ Fuck the Text, and if you're young, it's recent, and if you're older, it's either haunted you or has you questioning your own life's value. Try playing it as if you're remembering all this for the first time, and the splattered blood is the most beautiful thing you've ever seen; is that where your emotional 180 is? Try being really fascinated by it.

Play around with your moment after. You can try a long beat before the last line. You can say it and then look as if you have more to say, but stop yourself.

And who is she talking to? Is she confiding in a new lover? Is she telling her own child? Linda's brother? How is that person reacting? Is he or she comforting? Shocked? How does your relationship to the listener drive your words and instruct the way you perform this?

◇◇◇◇◇◇◇

⬦⬦⬦⬦⬦⬦

Monologue 10

That's what I didn't expect, though: the sound of trumpets. But I heard them. And there were the bright lights, everything. And Mom was there, and she looked so incredibly beautiful. I ran to her, and she hugged me so tight, but she whispered, "You're not done yet. You have to go back." I didn't want to. But I did. Here I am. And I feel so lost. I don't know what to do with myself, with my life . . . with you. I'm scared that if I let you in, you'll see everything in me and you won't like it and you'll leave me. Like everyone else does. I can't be alone again. I don't trust myself not to cut. It just feels too good. I watch the lines I draw heal, and it's like I'm controlling how I'm healing; I can see myself physically get better. As if the hospital, the doctors, as if they were all dreams, and I'm a normal person again. And I don't have to worry about a possible relapse, because I'm not crazy. I'm not crazy. I'm normal. And I can learn to breathe again. But in order to do that, I need you. I need you in my life. Don't go. Please, don't go. Not yet.

⬦⬦⬦⬦⬦⬦

◇◇◇◇◇◇◇

Helpful Direction

This character committed suicide and was brought back to life, but still has all the fears and depression from before. If being with the other person is the one way she'll feel safe and normal, she has to convince him or her to stay.

Who is the other character? Is it the sister/dad/stepdad/ex-boyfriend/husband/daughter/son/Fuck the Text, who can't deal with her problems? Where does the listener move to leave during her speech? If you find those specific moments, your character's next sentence has more immediacy and she has to figure out new tactics to get the person to stay. Does she make the other person feel guilt? Pity? Does she blame her situation on him or her? Play around with everything you can to increase the stakes.

And what does the listener do at the end? Does he or she leave? What's your moment after? Do you collapse into a ball? Do you scream? Play with the punctuation. Make this yours.

◇◇◇◇◇◇◇

SERIOCOMIC MONOLOGUES

◇◇◇◇◇◇◇

Monologue 11

Matt . . . I'm . . . I don't know what to say. What do you want me to say? You wouldn't have broken up with me if you'd known everything you know now? Matt . . . I mean, that's a line, right? We were so young. Of course you had to see what else was out there. I don't blame you for that. Matt. I'm getting married in two weeks . . . If I was single, I don't know. Probably. I mean, yeah, we'd probably talk about trying a relationship again, but you and I both know we would just start off having incredibly hot sex. Did I ever tell you I wrote an article about the perfect penis? Yeah. I once wrote an entire column about your dick.

◇◇◇◇◇◇◇

◇◇◇◇◇◇◇

Helpful Direction

This character goes through several weighty beat changes, including incredulousness, cynicism, forgiveness, duty; it's so meaty! Figure out what it is that's holding her back from getting together with him again. Or maybe she does! Does she still have feelings for him? Is she going to act on them? When you play around with it, what makes her story more interesting?

Play the confusion, the wanting, the reservations. There are a ton of beats in this one, a lot of subtext. When you finally get to the last line, play all the variations! Does she say it without being able to look at him because she's embarrassed? Does she say it with longing? Does she say it to make a point that he was the best? What would you do?

And if you don't like the last two lines because you're uncomfortable saying them, cut them. Change the line preceding them to something you would say in those given circumstances.

◇◇◇◇◇◇◇

◇◇◇◇◇◇

Monologue 12

I was talking to Josephine the other day, and she asked how you were doing. I said I didn't know. That I thought maybe you were keeping an arm's-length distance from me. Then I thought, well, why don't I just ask you? So. Are you? Because I understand if you are, I get it. I do. But. We were best friends. To go from that to . . . this. What is this? I miss you. I miss hugging you. This awkward do-we-or-don't-we-touch-each-other thing is exhausting. I love you. I still love you. I'm sorry I'm getting emotional. I miss us. I don't want an arm's-length distance between us. Unless it's right before we hug. Like this. Oh. Okay. No, I get it. I just . . .

◇◇◇◇◇◇

◇◇◇◇◇◇◇

Helpful Direction

When a relationship evolves so that best-friend lovers who can't keep their hands off each other become people who don't even hug anymore, a lengthy transitional period occurs that might be one of the saddest and most painful things we go through as women. It hurts. Feel the awkwardness, the yearning.

Who is this character? Were they going steady? Engaged? Married? What makes sense for your age?

There are several beats and emotional 180s to play around with here. How is she in the opening? Is she normal? Is everything fine? Is she nervous?

I think the important thing to think about with this piece is how scared she is to say what she's really feeling. How does that fear play out? Are there parts where she can laugh at herself? Where are the emotional 180s?

Admitting you still love the other person takes guts, and whenever one must be brave, emotions spill out. She asks for a hug, with her arms outstretched, and gets what is probably the exact opposite of what she thought would happen. How long does it take for her to realize the person isn't coming in for that hug, that truce? When she says she gets it, does she? Is she saying that to relieve the awkwardness? Do her emotions betray her? Is she crying?

Let your moment after hang in the air. Keep reacting. Know exactly what this person says to her after she's done talking and keep reacting to that.

◇◇◇◇◇◇◇

◇◇◇◇◇◇

Monologue 13

I don't know how to tell you I need more of your time without you getting upset. You turn into a teenager and immediately get defensive—you do! I'm not looking for a fight. I don't want to fight. See? My dukes are down. I'm just standing here, calmly, to tell you I'm not getting enough of your time. I need more of you. You got promoted, a big pay raise and reduced hours. You told me you were excited to reinvest in us. And I'm glad you've got more time to work on your personal projects, I am. I want you to do those things. But when you're not here at night, I am. By myself. Thinking about the bottles of wine we have. How I could open up a bottle and split it with you, just because. But by myself, a whole bottle is too much. And it just reminds me again that you're not here. I need more of you. Or I need to develop a drinking problem. Either/or. You're better on my liver, though, you know?

◇◇◇◇◇◇

◇◇◇◇◇◇◇

Helpful Direction

How scared is this character to even begin the conversation? What's her moment before? What did the other character say or do to make her start with those words? The joke is at the end of this piece, so the beginning must be an emotional 180 degrees away from that.

When she says she's not looking for a fight, it's a beautiful moment of someone just wanting to be understood. Play with the beat of her pointing out that her dukes are down. Show them being put down.

What emotions is she feeling when she says, "I need more of you"? Is she plaintive? Is she angry? Does she catch herself right after saying it, taken aback by how she sounds? Is she apologizing for a beat with just her eyes?

She's scared of being rejected, and she makes that joke at the end to ease the tension, a classic defense mechanism. Play the love. In a monologue, in a scene, in a play, always play the love. Stories are always about the relationships.

◇◇◇◇◇◇◇

∞∞∞∞∞

Monologue 14

What? Of course my marriage is okay! What a silly thing to ask! Why, is your marriage okay? I mean, why would you ask that? Did Robert say something to you? I mean, lately, yes, he's been working late, but everything is fine. You don't need to worry, trust me. Why would you ask that, though? You're on, what, your third divorce now? What could you possibly know about what it takes to make a relationship work when you can't even keep a husband? I'm sorry. I'm so sorry. I don't know what's wrong with me. I'm so on edge. Robert and I are separating and I'm falling apart.

∞∞∞∞∞

◇◇◇◇◇◇◇

Helpful Direction

It takes a lot of energy to pretend to the world that everything is okay when it's not.

This character has been holding secrets, and some of the intensity will come from her relationship with the other person. Who has she been lying to? Her mother? Her mother-in-law? Her sister? Best friend?

There are so many beats here; you could put a different intention behind almost every line, so take your time in between the sentences to allow an inner monologue where your character can process what she's just said and think about what she's going to say next. There isn't just one emotional 180 here; there are dozens. She's incredulous, she's pretending to be fine, she's attacking, she's apologizing. How and where do you personally play those objectives?

For the ending, feel free to take your time before admitting your relationship is over. Hiding it from your best friend/mom/mother-in-law/whoever has probably been incredibly taxing. Let that all come out on your last line.

Also, pretty much any time a character in a play or film or television show says, "What?" you can feel confident that they did in fact hear the other person; they're just processing the information themselves and don't like it. It's never "Could you speak up, please?" It's always "Why would you say that?"

◇◇◇◇◇◇◇

◇◇◇◇◇◇

Monologue 15

All right, Dean. We've been married five years now. It's been fun. But my eggs are about to explode. That's right. My eggs are about to explode because of our dishes. Yes, Dean. Take a look in that sink. It's full. Again. How? We are only two people! What are you doing that takes that many plates and bowls? Are you just grabbing them from the cupboards and putting them straight into the sink? Because I don't get it. I'll gladly trade for vacuum duty. And if you don't want to trade? I want a baby. Because in eight short years, we'll have a human dishwasher. A human vacuum cleaner! We're getting to that point where if we don't have a child soon, we might never have one. And I've always imagined being a mother, and I don't know what's going to happen to us if we don't have a child. A human Roomba, with your eyes.

◇◇◇◇◇◇

◇◇◇◇◇◇◇

Helpful Direction

I love pieces that read like nothing interesting is happening in them, because it usually means that people using that monologue didn't catch the drama in it. And this one is juicy! This character starts off fed up and making jokes, but then she says, "We're getting to the point where if we don't have a child soon, we might never have one." There's so much fear and vulnerability in that line and the line that follows. If you can get onto the verge of tears for those two lines, it's a beautiful emotional 180 that is going to take your auditors aback in wonderment.

For that last line, you can go back to trying to be funny again. Play around with the moment after; after making that joke, is she still upset? Is she plaintive? Laughing? Is she trying to show her partner she's fine, or not fine? What makes sense for your character? What makes sense for you?

◇◇◇◇◇◇◇

Monologue 16

Billy—what is that? Is that a . . . pit bull? You have a growling blue pit bull tattooed on your shoulder. It looks like garbage. Who did that to you? A friend just out of prison? Oh, my God. Oh, my God! I'm sorry I'm laughing, but oh, jeez, just go ahead and put your shirt back on. Sex is not happening tonight. Oh, good Lord! Why do you boys do this? Why do you guys get such stupid things permanently stained into your skin? I get it, you wanted to rebel, we all do, but all I can think, all we women can think, is how you put absolutely no forethought into what this ugly thing would look like to your future bedmates. And how that's probably a good indication of how you don't put any forethought into STDs or pregnancy prevention. Oh, my God. What am I doing? You're practically half my age. I'm so lonely. Billy. It's fine. Let's do this. I just . . . leave your shirt on, okay?

◇◇◇◇◇◇

Helpful Direction

I absolutely love how we start off fun and light and laughing, and then end on an existential crisis. Not what most auditors will expect!

Who is this woman? An older single lady? A fresh divorcée on the rebound? A woman who thought she had everything? . . . You?

Be committed with your choices regarding who she is, how she'd react, where she is, and who she's talking to. Who is Billy? A neighbor? A coworker? Her son's best friend? Her daughter's boyfriend? Play around with who he is to make sure the stakes are high for this character.

In your moment before, feel free to give a sense of environment by unbuttoning the top button of your blouse or jacket, or slipping your tank top strap off your shoulder. Then catch a glimpse of the tattoo and stop the physicality to focus on the words and laughing.

Once you get to "Oh my God," take your time. Have the crisis. This emotional 180-degree turn will captivate your audience. Play around with how you convince Billy that everything is okay at the end. Are you lighthearted again? Resigned? Ashamed? What works best for you?

Obviously, this piece can work great for women who could easily play a sexy mistress, but I also want to strongly encourage women who are older and think they're not the right type to try this out. It will be completely unexpected, and still so very honest and true. This piece highlights your vulnerability, which is such a gift to watch.

◇◇◇◇◇◇

◇◇◇◇◇◇

Monologue 17

There are two types of sexy based on what a woman drinks. The dirty-martini-drinking woman wears designer heels and has a confidence that oozes independence. The beer-drinking woman goes camping and looks sexy waking up. And then there's me. The water-no-ice girl. I am not sexy. I am always cold and high maintenance but think I'm not high maintenance, which is the absolute worst a woman can be. I have cellulite and stretch marks, and hairy legs because it's been so long since I've had sex that I've simply stopped bothering. I am not sexy. I'm clingy. And codependent. But I will be the best lay you've had in years because I need it so badly, so desperately. And I can drive you home 'cause I'm still sober. So pay your tab, give me your keys, and let's get the hell out of here already. Now.

◇◇◇◇◇◇

◇◇◇◇◇◇◇

Helpful Direction

You can play the no-nonsense woman who knows what she wants, or you can be geeky. Cater this character to the character you want to play in the project you're auditioning for. She could be any major archetype.

One of my favorite ways to play this is to have the character realize as she's talking that she's the water-no-ice girl. The discovery is always fun, as it can be tinged with self-loathing in the beginning but turn more confident and demanding at the end.

And, of course, what's your moment after here? Does he say yes? Are you grabbing your purse and heading out with him, or does he reject you? How do you take it? Give us some nonverbal acting brilliance!

◇◇◇◇◇◇◇

Monologue 18

I have something I want to say. When I first met Anthony, I thought, oh, it's not like I'm going to marry him. He was too handsome, too muscular, and, I thought, must be stupid. The last four years, I have constantly been surprised at how intelligent, how thoughtful, and how funny you are. We started out as an electronic match on a dating website and tomorrow will make it legal and binding in front of all our friends and family and God. You took this shy girl with a few silly dreams and showed her how to believe in herself and make her dreams a reality. I wouldn't have grown as much as I have without you by my side cheering me on. The very best thing about me, Anthony, is you. I love you. Here's to the next 100 years!

◇◇◇◇◇◇

Helpful Direction

Hey, look! A rehearsal dinner speech! Have you ever seen one? The bride always, always cries. Family members cry. Aww. So cute. And the best part? You don't have to think about your dead dog to get there. It's a happy cry! How do you perform it? By paying attention to the person you're speaking to! Put Anthony (or whatever his or her name is—Fuck the Text!) straight ahead, and when you talk about him to your family watching you, be sure to look around the room at them. By looking back and forth at the appropriate times, you'll create the family surrounding you and look fantastic doing it. It's playing with your environment!

If there's no emotional 180, this piece is boring, so think about your character; is she used to being the center of attention? Play around with how nervous she might be, and how she grows in confidence as she's talking about and to her fiancé. That's one way to get an emotional arc. Play around to see if there are any others.

Remember, Fuck the Text if you want to. If you want to describe the physicality of your own significant other, go for it! You know what else? It's perfectly acceptable to use your water bottle from your purse as a champagne glass.

◇◇◇◇◇◇

◇◇◇◇◇◇

Monologue 19

You're overreacting. Please calm down. Okay. I was at Joey's and everything was fine. He brought out some cheap wine, I said okay, and then he kept pouring. He kissed me. That's as far as it went. It wasn't pleasant, trust me. His tongue was—okay, no details. But my mouth was closed the whole time. I stopped it. I have no idea why he tried anything. He's not my type, and even if he was, there's you! There's God! And I know that! Nothing happened and he's incredibly embarrassed. It's probably best if you pretend you don't know. Well, I don't know, maybe confide to him that you never go in for a kiss with your tongue out of your mouth. Or, if he insists on that, to buy much better wine. I'm kidding!

◇◇◇◇◇◇

◇◇◇◇◇◇◇◇

Helpful Direction

Right off the bat, know who she's talking to. Her boyfriend? Her husband? Her mom? And who is Joey to that person? His best friend? His underachieving brother? Her stepson?

Now that you know the relationship between who you're talking to and who you're talking about, find your beats. In the opening, is she calm? Scared? Angry? What works for you? How does she calm the other person down when she shares her story? Is she joking at certain parts? Is she dead serious at others? How much does she go back and forth? How many emotional 180s does she have?

When she says the next-to-last line, is she saying that to the other person, or more to herself? How long a beat does she hold before she says she's just kidding at the end? Is she deadpan? Frustrated? Laughing?

Also, think about how you might Fuck the Text to make this piece more interesting. For instance, what if Joey was a girl? How does changing Joey's gender and name change the piece for you? What could you cut and change to make this piece more age appropriate?

◇◇◇◇◇◇◇◇

◇◇◇◇◇◇

Monologue 20

Well, that's a long story. My mother's crazy. And not that "Oh, my God, she calls me every day!" kind of crazy. I mean, she's really crazy. Like, lives in a twenty-four-hour care facility, crazy. It all started back when she blamed Pilgrims for things. Yeah, Pilgrims, I know. 'Cause if she had blamed anyone else, anyone else—Hispanics, black people—we could have been, "Mom is racist!" but no, she chose to pick on white people. Who've been dead for 400 years. And you know, I've been through therapy and such, so I've kinda come to terms with it and all, but every year, every Mother's Day, I'll go into a drugstore and take a look at the Hallmark cards, and none fit. They just don't seem right. "Mom, you've made me who I am today," "You, Mother, are the reason I achieve all that I do," "Mom, I love ya lots!" No, those just don't fit. 'Cause I'm always looking for one that I could get her. You know? Like "Well, Ma, you tried," or "Hey, Ma, no hard feelings." Maybe even "Thanks for expelling me from your womb one day." That sort of thing. But instead, while I'm looking for something to say, "Hey, Ma, don't worry, we're cool," instead, I just keep on getting reminded of what I didn't have and what everyone else, everyone else does. And I get a little angry. So, yeah. That's why I don't celebrate Thanksgiving.

◇◇◇◇◇◇

◇◇◇◇◇◇

Helpful Direction

The character's mother blamed Pilgrims for things, and that's why she doesn't celebrate Thanksgiving. Vocally highlight the word "Pilgrims" in the beginning so that, when given the punch line at the end, the audience isn't lost. And hell, if you can tell that the audience is a little lost, Fuck the Text and say, "'Cause of the, uh, Pilgrims."

This character is hiding her pain by being sarcastic and a little provocative, so if you can actually be near tears when you say, "And I get a little angry," you'll be fantastic. You're practically crying but saying you're angry, and there's such truth and beauty in that small moment. Take that beat. Milk it. Then brush yourself off and continue on with the punchline.

There's a lot of good stuff in here if you really tap into it, and I think you can. This one is really about knowing all your beats. There's a bunch.

◇◇◇◇◇◇

COMEDIC MONOLOGUES

◇◇◇◇◇◇

Monologue 21

If all these girls are going on these reality show competitions to be famous, why can't they be nice to each other? They're all there for the exact same thing! And when you find the girls who keep reiterating ad nauseam, "This is a competition! I am not here to make friends," I just want to slap them in their ridiculous faces! Would it kill you to drop the attitude and the insults? Why don't you be the nice girl everyone wants to be friends with? Bridget?! Get out of my room, fatty! Go away, you stupid pig! Ugh! I hate being interrupted. But yeah, those girls on those shows need an etiquette lesson on how to be nice to others. For reals.

◇◇◇◇◇◇

◇◇◇◇◇◇◇

Helpful Direction

Put Bridget (or whatever you want to call her) about a quarter turn to your side. That way, your face is still visible to the auditors. Placement is huge here. And play around with how your character gets the other person out of her space; does she rush through it? Does she pause between sentences? Does she try to make her feel especially unwanted with her tone, delivery, and perhaps a hand gesture shooing her out?

Also, who is Bridget? Your meddling and annoying baby sister? Your meek stepmom? How do these two different relationships affect how you get her out of your room?

◇◇◇◇◇◇◇

◇◇◇◇◇◇

Monologue 22

Oh, my God. That was terrible. He was so bad. Did you know he was this bad? What do we tell him when he sees us? We can't tell him the truth! What are we supposed to say? I mean, are my eyes bleeding? Blood had to have poured out my eyes, that was so godawful. Do we lie? Shut up! Shut up! He's coming right towards us! Hey, Matt! Oh, my gosh! You were in a play! You learned all those lines! Oh, my gosh, that set! And that one prop you had? You held on to that prop. So expertly. So good. Seriously, so good. Yeah, yeah, go ahead, say hi to your family, we'll be right here. Bye! John. Look at me. We cannot be his agents anymore.

◇◇◇◇◇◇

◇◇◇◇◇◇◇

Helpful Direction

We've all been there, haven't we? Where we support a friend in a play, a dance recital, a poetry reading, an art event, and . . . well. Yeah. Exactly. It sucks. But we still have to be their friend! And that's probably a good way to approach this piece.

Set up your environment and moment before, possibly by clapping for a few beats. Then, when that dies down, you lean over to John next to you, while still staring straight ahead.

If you decide that your character speaks to Matt really loudly and over the top, then the beginning and end need to be super understated. That's where the comedy truly is.

And how does she say those lines to Matt? Play around with saying each line differently, taking your time. She's stuck in a place of not wanting to lie, but also not wanting to hurt his feelings. Find your beats, and have an awesome time playing around with this.

◇◇◇◇◇◇◇

◇◇◇◇◇◇

Monologue 23

Hey, listen. We need to talk. Now, I know that's the scariest sentence anyone ever utters when they're in a relationship, but this isn't—I'm sorry. I didn't start off the way I wanted to. Okay. Uhh . . . Take two. Hey. Heeeeeey. I need to talk to you about something really important. See? Wasn't that better? You're not scared anymore, right? Okay, good. Good! So, yeah. Where was I? Right. We need to talk. No, babe! I'm sorry— gosh, um. Look, it's really not that bad. I swear. No, look! I'm crossing my heart! Okay? Good. We got this, honey. We're gonna get through this, okay? Nod your head with me. That's right. We're gonna get through this. It's truly not that big of a deal. Okay. All right. Okay. I don't want to be your girlfriend anymore.

◇◇◇◇◇◇

◇◇◇◇◇◇

Helpful Direction

I love this piece because there are so many levels and so many changes of direction here. She's sincere in her need to talk, but gets super uncomfortable when her invisible scene partner anticipates what's next. Her significant other might have already started crying, and she has to comfort him with her words and actions, but she still needs to break up. This puts her in such an awkward position, and the comedy comes out from the different emotions she experiences as she ping-pongs back and forth.

Find the beats where she's calming him down, and the ones where she's calming herself down. These types of conversations are never easy to have, and if you play up the nervousness at the end, I think you've got something pretty special.

Play around with the last line to see what works for you. Is she super serious? Is she still trying to soften the blow? What works best for your character? How does the other person react? How does your character then react to that?

◇◇◇◇◇◇

◇◇◇◇◇◇◇

Monologue 24

That is an excellent question. Just having watched how you and your partner interact shows me that, one: You have a shorthand which means there's no pressure of being politically correct in every interaction we might have, which saves us time, and I am a person who loves to work smarter, not harder; but also, two: That I want to be here. A female-run company where the leaders are fearless? You already act like your business is one of the top five in the industry, and even though you're boutique now, I completely foresee this company being a force to be reckoned with. Because how you act, how assertive, how commanding, how . . . formidable, is exactly how I would be. And bitches get shit done. Oh, gosh, I didn't mean to offend, I'm just—that's a meme? A famous meme all over social media a few years back, where powerful women are taking back the word "bitch" . . . So. Should I just go ahead and see myself out? Thank you for your time.

◇◇◇◇◇◇◇

◇◇◇◇◇◇

Helpful Direction

She is interviewing for a job. She is capable, she is brilliant, and this is the perfect company for her. The one she could see herself growing with and becoming a partner! She wants this! So when she says, "Bitches get shit done," implying her interviewer is a bitch, how does she try to recover? How does she show she knows she blew it? That the interview is over? On which lines do you make that clear?

There are definite beat changes here, so have fun playing around with all the different emotions that could happen in this piece.

Show your nonverbal acting brilliance after she asks if she should see herself out. Wait a beat and make a choice as to how the interviewer responds to that. Does she keep her on edge, waiting? Is she curt about it? Is she dismissive?

You can play this piece very realistically or very broadly. Whichever you choose, however, one fun way to approach the ending is if you pick up your purse and its contents fall out. Ad-lib whatever you would actually say in that situation, if you were that person in those given circumstances. Have some fun!

◇◇◇◇◇◇

◇◇◇◇◇◇

Monologue 25

Yes! Yes! That's exactly what's so creepy about those social networking sites where you need to post your relationship. When I changed my status to single, all of a sudden, and I mean all of a sudden, male friends I hadn't talked to in months were suddenly messaging and texting me, asking if I was all right. Boys just coming out of the woodwork to swoop in. Todd private messaged, "I know you must be hurting right now. Let me take you out for coffee." Mike texted, "I hope I can prove to you that not all guys are like your ex." And my favorite, from nerdy, awkward Chris, was "Sex tonight?" Straight to the point and with a dick pic. Like, what?! I mean, really! I should've said I broke up with my boyfriend long before my April Fool's Day prank on him. . . . And Chris? Wow.

◇◇◇◇◇◇

◇◇◇◇◇◇

Helpful Direction

She updated her social networking site status to "single" as an April Fool's joke on her boyfriend and she's suddenly bombarded with invitations and propositions.

Feel free to use your phone as a prop. It'll help ground the piece as you flip through and show proof of the messages.

If you're comfortable with it, Fuck the Text and use the names of real guys you know for the names of the guys in this piece. Consider finding little physical ways to help your friend know which guy you're talking about. If you decide that one of them is a gym rat, you could flex your arm when you talk about him. It's a small thing you can do with each guy that will help color your piece a little. And it's fun.

Play around with the idea that the character really is grossed out by all this unwanted attention, until she realizes in the moment that she should have broken up with her boyfriend long ago. And that last bit about Chris? Was what he did gross? Or did she sleep with him and it was amazing? What's funny to you? What works better for you?

◇◇◇◇◇◇

⬦⬦⬦⬦⬦⬦

Monologue 26

I was sitting at a seminar for this "How to Get the Life You Want" thing at a church I'm fairly certain is a cult. I know, I know, but they promised free cookies. I'm sitting in this very uncomfortable chair, and when the lights dim, there's this music that sounds very scary, high-pressure game-show, with the heartbeat and everything, you know? The room turns blue and this stuff starts coming out from these holes in the floor near our feet. I'm wondering if it's fog or poisonous gas, but then I thought, wait, of course they're not going to kill me because they want me to give them more of my money. And I was promised those cookies, you know? The music gets louder and louder and the heartbeat gets faster and faster and there's a loud cymbal crash and bam! White intense light! I'm blind! We're blind! And then the music stops and a loud voice booms over the speakers. . . . I don't remember exactly what it said, but there's another seminar that I'm totally going to. Do you want to come? There's free cookies and you get a whole bunch of pamphlets about the founder and how great he was. . . . They do gloss over how his gay son committed suicide because the founder would never accept him, but whatever, right? Hey! Wanna take a free personality test?

⬦⬦⬦⬦⬦⬦

◇◇◇◇◇◇◇

Helpful Direction

This character is fun because she really lives in the flashback—seriously, live it up! Try starting out normal, natural, and then, in the middle, going a little overboard like you would for Christopher Durang. Look at the fog swirling around your feet, be blinded by the bright white lights. And then, when she mentions that the son committed suicide, consider bringing it down, taking a beat to really feel sad for him. It really is that tragic. And then go back up to that same level of intensity because, oh, gosh, she really is excited about getting others to take that personality test.

Play around with that last line. Is she happy, mind-controlled? Is she super laser-focused and a little scary? What's funnier to you?

◇◇◇◇◇◇◇

◇◇◇◇◇◇

Monologue 27

I don't understand the point of all these hookup apps. I really don't. You see some stranger, swipe this way or that, go have drinks with them to see if they actually look like their photos, and then have sex with them? That sounds like so much work. Too much work. No, listen, Tanya, if you want dick, I have the foolproof way to get it. Okay, let's say you're in the fertile zone of your cycle and in need, right? Fine. Give me the name of one of your guy friends. Actually, let's just say Rick 'cause I know him from your housewarming party. He's the one who came with no date, right? Bought you that expensive bottle of champagne and a pot of succulents? You just text him, "Hey, we've been friends for a really long time, and you know what? I'd like to have sex with you if you're open to it." Works. Every. Time. Although, to be honest, it's a much better party trick in person. Their faces! First, they don't know if you're joking, and then they're sure you're joking, and then they see you're serious. Oh, it never gets old. I did that with all my coworkers at Cindy's going-away party. Fifteen dudes at my beck and call whenever I want. The only swiping I'm doing is of my dirty bits before they come over.

◇◇◇◇◇◇

~~~~~~~

Helpful Direction

What I love about this piece is how much *you* you get to bring to it. We all love telling people what to do, and we all have our particular ways of doing it. Some of us are insistent, some of us are a little more gentle, and some of us are super animated. Use your own personality to really make this piece great.

Fuck the Text if you don't like the name Tanya, and figure out who she is. Is she your best friend, college roommate, little sister, mom, daughter? Your relationship is going to dictate how you are in this piece. And when you start the piece, what is the moment before? Was Tanya in the middle of complaining about dating apps and your character is fed up, or is this a teaching moment? What's funnier? (I also truly love the idea of this monologue for an older actor trying to gross out her daughter. Change the coworkers to a knitting group, or whatever! Make this piece yours!)

This monologue has tons of room for levels, too. You get to go from fed up, to wise sage, to laughing and maybe even making faces, to sexually confident. Again, your personality is where the comedy lies here.

If you want to make it current, add the name of the app you want to talk about and then Fuck the Text to make it fit whatever parameters and features that app uses.

~~~~~~~

◇◇◇◇◇◇◇

Monologue 28

Hey, Addison, we need to have a serious roommate sit-down. Sit down, please. Addison. Sit down. Thank you. When we first started living together, we were both like, "What's mine is yours. Mi casa es su casa." But, um . . . Clothes, totally cool. Food? As long as it's not the last of it, or you immediately replace it before I come home from work, awesome. But, um. Gosh. How do I say this. Uh. My back massager . . . ? I don't, uh, use it to . . . massage my back. I know your job really sucks and you suffer from back pain, but . . . maybe . . . you get your own. Yeah. Yeah. Get your own.

◇◇◇◇◇◇◇

◇◇◇◇◇◇

Helpful Direction

Find your beats and emotional 180s. Where is this character nervous? Where is she adamant? Is she embarrassed? Find where she wants to tell her roommate the truth and then chickens out. Find different ways to play each of those instances.

You can absolutely take your time with this piece and let the different moments play out. Play with your tempo, your pace! Where is she slow? Where is she fast? Does she feel guilty about what she does, or does she feel guilty about not wanting her roommate to use her appliance, or both? What works best for you?

The punctuation is there as a guide. Take it out and change it if you don't like it or want to try it different ways.

◇◇◇◇◇◇

◇◇◇◇◇◇

Monologue 29

Remember Resting Bitch Face? Where some girls look mean or annoyed when they're just neutral? I have Tell Me All About Your Problems face. And it's way worse. I was waiting forever in line at the post office and this girl told me she thinks her boyfriend is cheating on her and listed all the reasons why. I was sweating on an elliptical and an older lady told me all about her hot flashes and hormone pills. I was at Starbucks, on my phone with my earphones plugged in, a hoodie over my head, with sunglasses on, and still was trapped into a conversation by some old hippie about astrology. For ten minutes. Why? Why must I have this face? All I'm thinking is, "Please, please, please stop! Why do you think I care?" But I don't say anything. I just nod pleasantly and "Uh huh," or "Mhmm." How can a face like this ever say "Shut the fu—Shut the fu—Shut the fu—" See? It can't. My face wants to hear your problems. . . . But my ears really don't.

◇◇◇◇◇◇

◇◇◇◇◇◇◇

Helpful Direction

Consider playing this character as prim and proper until she tries to say the f-word. Catch yourself, really chew on the "fu" the second time, and then screw your face up with all your might on the last "fu—" to really drive that point home. Then go back to your prim and proper self. In fact, maybe she even whispers the word "bitch" in the first line. Play around with it.

Anytime there's a list in a monologue, you have to say each item in the list differently. Lists of three items are usually setting up a punchline. You can play up how you were at the Starbucks, displaying all the indications that you weren't interested in conversation, and how crazy it was that it was still initiated. That's also a pretty great spot to elevate the physical comedy by being a little louder and bigger with your words and actions. For instance, if you choose to have your emotional 180 there, the beginning and end can be nice, sweet little bookends.

◇◇◇◇◇◇◇

∞∞∞∞∞

Monologue 30

It's not my fault, Olivia! It's those Silicon Valley nerds who keep inventing new social networking sites—it's their fault I'm unintentionally stalking my ex-boyfriend. Last week Adam tweeted that he was at a new club with an "amazing lady." Those nerds knows I'm a follower and can read that! And then he flirted with her on Facebook, where everyone can see what he writes, and he and Mystery Flirty Lady have an entire exchange where they go on and on with the innuendoes—and the nerds push his status to the top of my feed with each and every one of their comments! They make me know what Adam's doing! They make sure I can see his check-ins and Yelp reviews and know exactly where he's been and where he's at, at any moment! The Silicon Valley nerds want me to be a psycho ex-girlfriend! I'm not a psycho ex-girlfriend! I'm not, Olivia! Oh, God. I am! I have to delete all my accounts! I have to delete everything. But then I won't know what he's doing! What am I going to do?

∞∞∞∞∞

◇◇◇◇◇◇

Helpful Direction

This is a monologue about social networking sites, and every five years or so a new one will pop up and take over the world, so Fuck the Text and change the wording to fit the current times.

This is another monologue where you can play the humor with subtlety or can go all-out crazy. Master both ways and you'll have a great comedic and seriocomic piece. Know your beats, know your emotional 180s, and find the fun. When she realizes that she is in fact the psycho ex-girlfriend, have her discover it as she's saying it. That's a really funny moment, especially because she can have her emotional 180 right after it—and, quite possibly, one more time after that.

◇◇◇◇◇◇

Afterword

Whew! There you go! Thirty monologues with advice, tips, and helpful direction, all to help you be the best actor you can be. I hope you found this book beneficial, and I hope you find yourself growing as a storyteller, thinking about character aspects you might not have considered before. With practice, rehearsal, and dedication, that skill will become second nature.

We actors are a special group of people, aren't we? Thank you for letting me come into your life. I wish you all the happiness and success you desire.

You can do it.

Monologue and Scene Books

Best Contemporary Monologues for Kids Ages 7-15
edited by
Lawrence Harbison
9781495011771 .... $16.99

Best Contemporary Monologues for Men 18-35
edited by
Lawrence Harbison
9781480369610 .... $16.99

Best Contemporary Monologues for Women 18-35
edited by
Lawrence Harbison
9781480369627 .... $16.99

Best Monologues from The Best American Short Plays, Volume Three
edited by
William W. Demastes
9781480397408 .... $19.99

Best Monologues from The Best American Short Plays, Volume Two
edited by
William W. Demastes
9781480385481 .... $19.99

Best Monologues from The Best American Short Plays, Volume One
edited by
William W. Demastes
9781480331556 .... $19.99

The Best Scenes for Kids Ages 7-15
edited by
Lawrence Harbison
9781495011795 .... $16.99

Childsplay
A Collection of Scenes and Monologues for Children
edited by Kerry Muir
9780879101886 .... $16.99

Duo!: The Best Scenes for Mature Actors
edited by Stephen Fife
9781480360204 .... $19.99

Duo!: The Best Scenes for Two for the 21st Century
edited by Joyce E. Henry, Rebecca Dunn Jaroff, and Bob Shuman
9781557837028 .... $19.99

Duo!: Best Scenes for the 90's
edited by John Horvath, Lavonne Mueller, and Jack Temchin
9781557830302 .... $18.99

In Performance: Contemporary Monologues for Teens
by JV Mercanti
9781480396616 .... $16.99

In Performance: Contemporary Monologues for Men and Women Late Teens to Twenties
by JV Mercanti
9781480331570 .... $18.99

In Performance: Contemporary Monologues for Men and Women Late Twenties to Thirties
by JV Mercanti
9781480367470 .... $16.99

Men's Comedic Monologues That Are Actually Funny
edited by Alisha Gaddis
9781480396814 .... $14.99

One on One: The Best Men's Monologues for the 21st Century
edited by Joyce E. Henry, Rebecca Dunn Jaroff, and Bob Shuman
9781557837011 .... $18.99

One on One: The Best Women's Monologues for the 21st Century
edited by Joyce E. Henry, Rebecca Dunn Jaroff, and Bob Shuman
9781557837004 .... $18.99

One on One: The Best Men's Monologues for the Nineties
edited by Jack Temchin
9781557831514 .... $12.95

One on One: The Best Women's Monologues for the Nineties
edited by Jack Temchin
9781557831521 .... $11.95

One on One: Playing with a Purpose
Monologues for Kids Ages 7-15
edited by Stephen Fife and Bob Shuman with contribuing editors Eloise Rollins-Fife and Marit Shuman
9781557838414 .... $16.99

One on One: The Best Monologues for Mature Actors
edited by Stephen Fife
9781480360198 .... $19.99

Scenes and Monologues of Spiritual Experience from the Best Contemporary Plays
edited by Roger Ellis
9731480331563 .... $19.99

Scenes and Monologues from Steinberg/ATCA New Play Award Finalists, 2008-2012
edited by Bruce Burgun
9781476868783 .... $19.99

Soliloquy!
The Shakespeare Monologues
edited by Michael Earley and Philippa Keil
9780936839783
Men's Edition $12.99
9780936839790
Women's Edition $14.95

Teen Boys' Comedic Monologues That Are Actually Funny
edited by Alisha Gaddis
9781480396791 .... $14.99

Teens Girls' Comedic Monologues That Are Actually Funny
edited by Alisha Gaddis
9781480396807 .... $14.99

Women's Comedic Monologues That Are Actually Funny
edited by Alisha Gaddis
9781480360426 ...... $14.99

www.halleonardbooks.com

More Titles from The Applause Acting Series

How I Did It
Establishing a Playwriting
Career
edited by Lawrence Harbison
9781480369634...............$24.99

**25 10-Minute Plays
for Teens**
edited by Lawrence Harbison
9781480387768...............$16.99

**More 10-Minute Plays
for Teens**
edited by Lawrence Harbison
9781495011801..................$9.99

10-Minute Plays for Kids
edited by Lawrence Harbison
9781495053399..................$9.99

On Singing Onstage
by David Craig
9781557830432...............$18.99

**The Stanislavsky
Technique: Russia**
by Mel Gordon
9780936839080...............$16.95

Speak with Distinction
by Edith Skinner/Revised with
New Material Added by Timothy
Monich and Lilene Mansell
9781557830470...............$39.99

Recycling Shakespeare
by Charles Marowitz
9781557830944...............$14.95

Acting in Film
by Michael Caine
9781557832771...............$19.99

The Actor and the Text
by Cicely Berry
9781557831385...............$22.99

**The Craftsmen
of Dionysus**
by Jerome Rockwood
9781557831552...............$19.99

A Performer Prepares
by David Craig
9781557833952...............$19.99

Directing the Action
by Charles Marowitz
9781557830722...............$18.99

**Acting in Restoration
Comedy**
by Simon Callow
9781557831194...............$18.99

**Shakespeare's Plays
in Performance**
by John Russell Brown
9781557831361...............$18.99

The Shakespeare Audition
How to Get Over Your Fear,
Find the Right Piece, and
Have a Great Audition
by Laura Wayth
9781495010804...............$16.99

OTHER ACTING TITLES AVAILABLE

The Monologue Audition
A Practical Guide for Actors
by Karen Kohlhaas
9780879102913...............$22.99

The Scene Study Book
Roadmap to Success
by Bruce Miller
9780879103712...............$16.99

Acting Solo
Roadmap to Success
by Bruce Miller
9780879103750...............$16.99

Actor's Alchemy
Finding the Gold in the Script
by Bruce Miller
9780879103835...............$16.99

**Stella Adler – The Art
of Acting**
compiled & edited by
Howard Kissel
9781557833730...............$29.99

Acting with Adler
by Joanna Rotté
9780879102982...............$16.99

Accents
A Manual for Actors –
Revised & Expanded Edition
by Robert Blumenfeld
9780879109677...............$29.99

Acting with the Voice
The Art of Recording Books
by Robert Blumenfeld
9780879103019...............$19.95

AN IMPRINT OF
HAL•LEONARD®
www.halleonardbooks.com

Prices, contents, and availability subject to change without notice.